J
BIO
NIXON

Ochester, Betsy

Richard M. Nixon
    Encyclopedia of presidents

Richard M. Nixon

Richard M. Nixon

Betsy Ochester

AMERICA'S
37TH
PRESIDENT

Children's Press®
A Division of Scholastic Inc.
New York / Toronto / London / Auckland / Sydney
Mexico City / New Delhi / Hong Kong
Danbury, Connecticut

Library of Congress Cataloging-in-Publication Data

Ochester, Betsy.
    Richard M. Nixon / Betsy Ochester.
      p. cm. — (Encyclopedia of presidents. Second series)
    Includes bibliographical references (p.   ) and index.
 ISBN 0-516-22978-8
   1. Nixon, Richard M. (Richard Milhous), 1913–1994—Juvenile literature.
2. Presidents—United States—Biography—Juvenile literature. I. Title. II.
Encyclopedia of presidents (2003)
E856.O26 2005
973.924'092—dc22   2004017724

Contents

One   7
Family Ties

Two   21
War and Politics

Three   35
Second in Command

Four   51
Triumph

Five   73
Scandal

Six   87
The Final Comeback

Presidential Fast Facts   96
First Lady Fast Facts   97
Timeline   98
Glossary   100
Further Reading   101
Places to Visit   102
Online Sites of Interest   103
Table of Presidents   104
Index   108

Chapter 1

August 9, 1974

On the South Lawn of the White House, a long red carpet stretched out toward a waiting presidential helicopter. The president and his family prepared to walk out to the helicopter, flanked by a military honor guard. To a casual observer, the scene might have seemed routine, resembling dozens of other presidential departures. This time, it was anything but routine.

That morning, President Richard M. Nixon had become the first president ever to resign from office. Now, while millions watched on television, Nixon shook hands with Gerald Ford, who would soon be sworn in as the next president. Then he followed his family up the stairs to the helicopter. On the top step, he stopped and turned to face those gathered below. He waved his right arm in a full-sweeping good-bye, then raised both arms above his head and extended the first

Nixon waves farewell from the steps of the helicopter on the White House lawn on August 9, 1974.

two fingers on each hand in his familiar V-for-victory sign. His face lit up in a huge smile.

Then Nixon disappeared into the helicopter. Soon afterward, he and his family were on their way to the Nixons' estate in Southern California, marking the end of Richard Nixon's public political career. Many in the country cheered his departure, relieved that Nixon was gone from power. A few of his faithful supporters were angry, believing he had been unfairly persecuted. Through his long career, Richard Nixon evoked powerful emotions from critics and supporters alike.

As the Nixon family flew high above the nation's heartland, Gerald Ford was sworn in as president. He began his brief inaugural remarks with these words: "Our long national nightmare is over."

Why had President Nixon resigned with more than two years left in his term? What "nightmare" was Ford referring to? Born in humble circumstances, Nixon showed grit and determination, refusing to quit even after discouraging defeats, and gaining election to the highest office in the land. He became an innovative president and an admired world leader, but his combative and suspicious nature betrayed him, bringing disgrace and resignation. The story of his rise and fall begins in the open spaces of Southern California, then still sparsely populated and seemingly far from the center of American power.

"A Drive to Succeed"

Richard Milhous Nixon was born in Yorba Linda, California, on January 9, 1913, in a modest house his father built. He was a large baby, weighing 11 pounds (5 kilograms), with a "powerful, ringing voice," according to the nurse who helped deliver him. The second of five boys born to Frank and Hannah Nixon, Nixon was named for Richard the Lion-Hearted, king of England. His middle name, Milhous, was his mother's maiden name.

Yorba Linda was a small settlement near Los Angeles surrounded by citrus groves. Frank Nixon owned a 13-acre (5.2-hectare) lemon farm. It wasn't profitable, and the family struggled to make ends meet. Nixon recalled that during his childhood his mother never had a new dress, and the family never ate at a restaurant or took a vacation.

Richard shared a bedroom with his three brothers, Harold, Donald, and Arthur. (The youngest son, Edward, was born when Richard was 17.) Richard was a thoughtful, serious boy. While his brothers were eager to play games and have fun, Richard was often reading a book. Early in life, he began to dream of traveling to see the wider world. "As a young boy," he later recalled, "sometimes at night I was awakened by the sound of a train whistle, and I would dream of the far-off places I wanted to visit someday." He used to pore over an aunt's *National Geographic* magazines and imagine being in the exotic places described.

The house in Yorba Linda, California, where Richard Nixon was born in 1913. Today it is part of the Richard Nixon Presidential Library.

Frank and Hannah Nixon had temperaments as different as night and day. Frank was loud, aggressive, and quick to anger. One day, when he caught Harold and Richard swimming in a canal against his strict orders, he yanked the two out of the canal, then flung them back in, shouting, "Do you like water? Have some more of it!" Hannah, a devout Quaker, was calm and quiet. The Quaker religion played a large role in the Nixon household. Quakers were austere, hardworking people, who didn't believe in dancing or drinking alcohol. Many Quakers were also *pacifists*, opposed to supporting or fighting in wars. Hannah, though a kind woman, was reserved with her boys, rarely giving them hugs or kisses, or saying, "I love you."

Both parents encouraged their boys to think big. "There was a drive to succeed," Richard later said. "My mother and father instilled in us the desire to . . . be good not just at one single thing but at everything." Richard took that desire to heart.

Hannah taught him to read at age five, and by the time he was six, Richard was reading newspapers and discussing current events with his father. His first-grade teacher said of him, "He absorbed knowledge of every kind like a blotter." On her recommendation, he skipped second grade.

In 1922, when Richard was nine, the family moved to the nearby Quaker town of Whittier. They lived in another house that Frank built. Yearning to run his

The Nixon family in 1916: parents Frank and Hannah and sons Harold, Donald, and Richard. Two more sons were born later.

own business, Frank opened a gasoline station. When a new Quaker meeting-house was built in town, Frank bought the old one. He had it moved to his property and turned it into a grocery store. Frank, Hannah, and all the boys worked hard in the Nixon Market. Hannah baked dozens of pies to sell each day, and the boys helped out when they weren't in school.

When Richard was twelve, tragedy struck the Nixon family. His youngest brother, seven-year-old Arthur, became ill and died of an infection in August 1925. Richard was devastated. He later wrote, "For weeks after Arthur's funeral, there was not a day that I did not think about him and cry." Arthur's death, Hannah said, made Richard want to succeed even more, as if he were trying to replace his parents' pain with pride in his own success.

Keeping Busy

In the fall of 1926, Richard entered high school in the nearby town of Fullerton. Two years later, he transferred to Whittier High School. Dick, as everyone but his mother called him, joined many activities in high school. He was a member of the Latin club, the school newspaper, and the orchestra. He acted in school plays and went out for football, basketball, and track. Although he never made the starting teams, Dick always showed up for practice. His greatest accomplishments came in debate. Though shy when talking with a small group, Dick was confident and outgoing when talking to a larger audience. Formal debating came naturally to him, and he was soon skilled at taking either side of an argument. Dick led his debating team to regional and state championships.

At the same time, Dick continued to work at the Nixon store. When he got his driver's license, he got up at 4 a.m. each day, drove to Los Angeles to buy fruits and vegetables at the farmers' market, then set them out for display on the store's counters—all before he left for school.

Richard Nixon became a top student and a star debater in high school and at Whittier College.

During Dick's high school years, the family suffered another blow. Dick's older brother Harold contracted tuberculosis, a disease of the lungs that was then usually incurable. Doctors suggested that a dry mountain climate might help Harold recover. Hannah left the rest of the family in Whittier and took Harold to Prescott, Arizona. There she rented a small cabin and housed three other tuberculosis patients, cooking, cleaning, and tending to all four.

Over school breaks, Dick visited Hannah and Harold in Prescott. In 1930, Hannah returned to Whittier, where she gave birth to her fifth son, Edward. Not long afterward, Harold also returned home to Whittier.

Three Sons in One ———————————————

Richard Nixon had dreams of going to college in the East. He won an award from the Harvard Club of California that qualified him for a scholarship to Harvard University. The scholarship covered only tuition, however. Dick knew that his family could not afford his room and board and travel expenses, so he did not apply. Instead, he enrolled at nearby Whittier College, a school founded by Quakers, and continued to live at home.

In college, Nixon participated in many activities. He was elected president of his freshman class and later student body president. In addition, he was a reporter for the campus newspaper, a member of the debate club and the football team, and an actor in school plays. He also continued to make the vegetable run for the Nixon store.

Although popular on campus, Dick didn't have many close friends. Two important people were his high school sweetheart, whom he continued to date throughout college, and his football coach, Wallace Newman. Nixon gave

A Square Shooter

When Dick Nixon arrived on the campus of Whittier College in 1930, he was asked to join a new men's social club. He joined and soon made himself so useful that he was elected its first president. Club members called themselves the Orthogonians, which means "square shooters." Most members were athletes or students who were working their way through college. They provided competition to the Franklins, a social club for men from prominent or wealthy families. For the yearbook photograph, the Franklins wore tuxedos, while the Orthogonians wore open-necked shirts. Dick Nixon identified with the Orthogonians and resented the wealthy Franklins. He was proud to be a self-made man who worked for his success. This would become a familiar theme throughout his life.

☆ ★ ☆

Newman credit for instilling in him "a competitive spirit and the determination to come back after you have been knocked down or after you lose."

Meanwhile, Harold's condition was getting worse. On March 7, 1933, Richard received a message at the college to come home. He arrived to find a hearse in the driveway. Harold had died that morning. Richard sank into a deep depression. From then on, Hannah said, "it seemed that Richard was trying to be *three* sons in one, striving even harder than before to make up to his father and me for our loss."

Nixon graduated second in his college class and won a scholarship to law school at Duke University in North Carolina. In a recommendation to Duke, Whittier College's president wrote: "I cannot recommend him too highly because I believe that Nixon will become one of America's important, if not great, leaders."

Nixon takes a serious pose as a first-year law student at Duke University.

Law School

Nixon arrived on Duke's campus in the fall of 1934, in the heart of the Great Depression. Economic times were terrible. Fifteen million Americans were unemployed, and thousands of families were homeless and hungry, living in shanty-towns and depending on charity handouts for food. Business was poor for the Nixon store, too. Richard Nixon knew that he would have to do well and keep his scholarship. Without it, he would have to drop out of school. He soon learned that doing well would be a challenge because standards were higher and competition was sharper in the law school than in college. He kept up by working harder than ever. Fellow students nicknamed him "Gloomy Gus" for his seriousness and "Iron-Butt" for his ability to sit and study for hours at a time. He did make some time for fun though, playing handball each afternoon and cheering himself hoarse at football games.

In the spring of 1937, Nixon's parents, grandmother, and young brother Edward drove all the way from California to North Carolina to see him graduate from the Duke Law School third in his class. He applied to a few New York City law firms for a job, but he received no offers.

The New Deal

In 1932, as the Depression reached a low point, Democrat Franklin D. Roosevelt was elected president, promising a "New Deal" to address the economic downturn and the suffering of millions of citizens. He passed sweeping measures, creating new government-sponsored jobs, assisting industry and farmers, and establishing social programs to help poor Americans. The New Deal brought relief to millions, but it did not end the Depression, which dragged on through the 1930s.

Republicans criticized Roosevelt's New Deal for putting too much power in the government's hands, and they accused Roosevelt of wanting dictatorial powers. Nixon himself would criticize the New Deal's faith in big government, but he recognized that it had permanently changed the government's role in American life.

☆ ★ ☆

The dean of the law school, who knew that Nixon was interested in public office, gave the young graduate some advice. "If you're going into politics, go back to your hometown and establish yourself in a law firm."

That's exactly what Nixon did.

Chapter 2

Love at First Sight

As soon as Richard Nixon laid eyes on Pat Ryan, he knew he'd found the love of his life. The two were auditioning for a play at a local theater in Whittier. Nixon immediately felt drawn to the slender redhead. When the audition was over, he offered Pat and her girlfriend a ride home. During the trip, he mustered up his courage and said to Pat, "I'd like to have a date with you."

Pat laughed and replied, "Oh, I'm too busy."

Nixon asked again at the first play rehearsal, but again she said no. On their third meeting, Dick asked, "When are you going to give me that date?" Pat laughed. Nixon pointed his finger at her, "Don't laugh," he said. "Someday I'm going to marry you." Pat was shocked and laughed even harder, but she did finally agree to a date.

Patricia Ryan

Like her future husband, Pat Ryan had grown up knowing hard work and difficult times. She was born Thelma Catherine Ryan on March 16, 1912, in Ely, Nevada, the daughter of an unsuccessful copper miner. Because she was born on the eve of St. Patrick's Day, her Irish father always called her "Pat," and she later legally changed her name to Patricia. The family moved to Southern California when Pat was two years old. When she was 13, her mother died, leaving Pat to take care of her father and two brothers, doing all the cooking, sewing, and cleaning. Yet she found time to earn excellent grades and be involved school activities, including debating and acting.

Pat Ryan, an attractive and independent young woman, first met Nixon in 1937. They were married in June 1940.

When she graduated from high school, Pat had to stay home to nurse her father, who had contracted tuberculosis. He died the following year, and Pat moved to New York City. Three years later, she returned and enrolled as a 21-year-old freshman at the University of Southern California in Los Angeles, paying her way with many part-time jobs. She graduated with honors in 1937 and took a job teaching business education at Whittier High School. Soon afterward she met Richard Nixon.

☆☆☆

Both Dick and Pat lived in Whittier. Pat was a teacher at Whittier High School, and Nixon had joined the small law firm of Wingert and Bewley after gaining his law license. He spent much of his time on minor cases, but his careful work habits earned the respect of his colleagues. After less than two years, Nixon was made a partner in the firm.

Before long, Pat became fond of Dick Nixon, with his dark curly hair, his romantic notes, and his drive to succeed. After they had dated for two years, Dick drove Pat to Dana Point, a rocky bluff high above the Pacific Ocean. As the sun was setting, he asked Pat to marry him. She said yes, and they were married on June 21, 1940, in Riverside, California.

Lieutenant "Nick" ———————————————

On December 7, 1941, the Japanese staged a surprise attack on the American naval base at Pearl Harbor in Hawaii, and the next day the United States declared war. Soon afterward, Dick and Pat Nixon moved to Washington, D.C., where Nixon took a job with a wartime government agency. The new position gave Nixon a chance to learn firsthand how the federal government worked, but he soon found it dull.

Meanwhile, the United States began calling up draftees for military duty. Thousands of others rushed to enlist. Nixon felt an obligation to serve his country in

Fast Facts

What: War involving most of the countries of the world, between the Axis powers and the Allied powers

When: 1939–1945

Who: The Axis powers included Germany, Italy, and Japan. The Allied powers included Britain, France, the Soviet Union, the United States, China, Australia, Canada, and many other nations.

Where: In Europe (including the Soviet Union), North Africa, and Asia, and on the Atlantic and Pacific Oceans

Why: The Axis powers attacked neighboring countries, seeking world domination, territory for expansion, and natural resources.

Outcome: Allied forces gradually recovered territories conquered by the Axis, then attacked the Axis countries themselves. Italy surrendered in 1943. Germany surrendered May 7, 1945, after Allied forces entered Berlin, the German capital. Japan surrendered August 14, 1945, after the U.S. dropped atomic bombs on the Japanese cities of Hiroshima and Nagasaki. Germany was occupied by the main Allied powers, and Japan was governed by U.S. occupation forces.

wartime, and he knew that serving would be important to his political future. He enlisted in the navy in June 1942 and entered officer training. He was commissioned a lieutenant and was soon shipped to the South Pacific, where U.S. forces were fighting the Japanese.

Stationed first on the island of New Caledonia and later on the Solomon Islands, Nixon worked for a naval air transport unit, supervising the loading and unloading of large cargo planes. In the Solomons, his base was shelled by the Japanese for 28 out of 30 nights. That was the closest he came to combat. Nixon's transport unit had an important role to play, however, and he became a popular and effective junior officer. He opened Nick's Snack Shack, where he served free hamburgers and beer that he had scrounged from military supplies. He also learned to play poker, and discovered he had a talent for the game. He left the navy with thousands of dollars in winnings, which he used to help finance his first political campaign. Despite his success, he missed Pat terribly, and the two wrote to each other every day.

Nixon was transferred in July 1944 to duty at naval bases in the United States. In 1945, as the war came to an end, Nixon was discharged from the navy.

Dick Nixon was a popular junior officer during his navy service in the South Pacific during World War II.

A "Rocking, Socking Campaign"

In September 1945, Richard Nixon received a letter from a group of California businessmen who supported Republican candidates for office. They asked if Nixon was interested in running for the U.S. House of Representatives in the district that included Whittier. Nixon eagerly said yes, and he and Pat moved back to Whitter. They set up a campaign office in an old storefront, and Pat served as the only full-time campaign worker. She took time out only to give birth to their first daughter, Tricia, returning to the office three weeks later.

Nixon had an uphill battle and he promised to run a "rocking, socking campaign." He was running against Jerry Voorhis, a popular Democrat who had held the seat for nearly ten years. Yet Nixon knew that many people were blaming the Democrats for a business slowdown after the war and felt it was time for a change. As he traveled the district, sometimes wearing his navy uniform, he impressed local Republicans.

A major concern in 1946 was the threat of Communist countries, especially the power of the Soviet Union (which included present-day Russia and several smaller surrounding states). The Soviets and the United States had been allies during the war against Germany, but now the Soviets were establishing Communist governments in Eastern Europe and Asia. There was also evidence that they were spying on the United States.

Nixon exploited people's fear of Communists. He charged falsely that Voorhis had Communist ties in his background. In a public debate, Nixon pointed to Voorhis's voting record in Congress, suggesting that Voorhis was "soft" on Communism. Nixon caught his opponent by surprise, and Voorhis stumbled on his answer. After that, Voorhis was unable to shake the public's belief that he had Communist sympathies. Even old friends of Nixon were shocked by his aggressive attack. On election day Nixon won 57 percent of the vote against the popular

YOUR VETERAN CANDIDATE

Dick Nixon is a serious, energetic individual with a high purpose in life—to serve his fellow man. He is a trained scholar, a natural leader and a combat war veteran. He has acquired the "human touch" the hard way—by working his way through college and law school; by sleeping in fox-holes, sweating out air raids; by returning from war confronted with the necessity of "starting all over again."

There is in Richard Nixon's background much that is typical of the young western American. There are the parents from the mid-west, the father who has been street car motorman, oil field worker, citrus rancher, grocer. There is the solid heritage of the Quaker faith; the family tradition of Work—and Service.

The effects of this background show in Richard Nixon. He has worked in a fruit packing house, in stores, as a gas station attendant. He has made an outstanding success of his law practice. He played college football ("not too successfully," he says); maintains an intensive interest in sports.

Of course, the No. 1 Nixon-for-Congress enthusiasts are Mrs. Richard Nixon, born Patricia Ryan on St. Patrick's Day, and six-months-old baby daughter Pat. Mrs. Nixon is a public servant in her own right, having worked for the government as an economist while her husband was fighting for his country in the South Pacific. Like so many other young "war couples," the Nixons resumed civilian life on a financial foundation comprised solely of War Bonds purchased from the savings of the working wife and sailor husband.

Mr. and Mrs. Richard Nixon have been very busy this year. Individually or jointly, they have (1) been looking for a place to live; (2) practiced law; (3) been taking care of their little girl; (4) been active in veterans' affairs, particularly those relating to housing for Whittier College veteran-students and their families; (5) been looking for a place to live again; and (6) they have been campaigning to ELECT RICHARD M. NIXON TO CONGRESS.

For New, Progressive, Representation in Congress

VOTE FOR

RICHARD M. NIXON

ON NOVEMBER 5

MR. AND MRS. RICHARD M. NIXON AND PATRICIA

"I pledge myself to serve you faithfully;

To act in the best interests of all of you;

To work for the re-dedication of the United States of America as a land of opportunity for your children and mine;

To resist with all my power the encroachments of foreign isms upon the American way of life;

To preserve our sacred heritages, in the name of my buddies and your loved ones, who died that these might endure;

To devote my full energies to service for you while opposing regimentation of you;

To remain always humble in the knowledge of your trust in me."

Richard M. Nixon

ELECT

RICHARD M.
NIXON
WORLD WAR II VETERAN

YOUR CONGRESSMAN

Part of a flyer issued by Nixon's 1946 campaign for Congress.

Voorhis. He later recalled, "Nothing could equal the excitement of . . . winning the first campaign. Pat and I were happier on November 6, 1946, than we were ever to be again in my political career."

"Intensely Sincere"

Dick, Pat, and baby Tricia moved to Washington, D.C., where Dick was sworn in as a congressman in January 1947. The young, eager Republican could not have picked a better time to begin his political career. For the first time in 16 years, Republicans outnumbered Democrats in both the House and the Senate. This gave Nixon a chance to play a larger role in forming policy. He was ready. *Newsweek* magazine called him "intensely sincere" and "deeply impressive."

In 1947, he was one of 19 congressmen chosen to travel to Europe to survey the damage inflicted by World War II. When he saw the terrible destruction there, he concluded that without American aid, millions would starve and democratic governments might not survive. He became a strong supporter of the Marshall Plan (named for Secretary of State George Marshall) to provide billions of U.S. dollars to help rebuild the war-torn countries of Europe. Many Republicans were opposed to the huge foreign-aid program, but it passed and was highly successful. Nixon remained a firm *internationalist*, favoring U.S. involvement with other nations.

The Cold War

The competition between the United States and the Soviet Union raged through most of Richard Nixon's career, and became known as the Cold War. Unlike a "hot war," the Cold War did not involve major wars. Instead, it was a competition between two political and economic systems. Following the policies of Marxist *Communism*, the Soviet government controlled all property, industries, and businesses in the name of the people. In its elections, there was only one political party, the Communist party. Communist leaders believed that this form of government would one day take over the world. The United States and its allies favored private ownership of property and businesses, personal freedoms, and competitive elections in which voters had a choice.

After the Soviet Union exploded its first nuclear weapon in 1949, the two great powers began a long arms race, each producing huge stockpiles of weapons to guard against war with the other. At the same time, they sought alliances with nations not aligned with either side. This led to fierce economic competition and to localized wars in Korea (1950–1953), Vietnam (1953–1975), and elsewhere.

Richard Nixon made his political reputation as an anti-Communist, but later as president, he led efforts to achieve *détente*, an easing of tensions between the two superpowers. Between 1989 and 1991, people in Communist countries revolted against their governments, and in 1991 the Soviet Union was dissolved, ending the Cold War.

The Hiss Case ——————————————

Nixon was assigned by House leaders to the House Un-American Activities Committee (HUAC), which investigated *subversives*, Communists and others with antigovernment views, who might seek to undermine government operations. Nixon's work on this committee helped make his national reputation.

In August 1948, HUAC began investigating Alger Hiss, a lawyer who had served in the U.S. State Department. Hiss was accused being a Communist and sending secret government information to the Soviet Union during his years in government service. Hiss's many friends and supporters considered the charge preposterous, but his accuser, Whittaker Chambers, claimed he had worked with Hiss to deliver the documents to Soviet agents.

At first, Hiss swore under oath that he did not know Whittaker Chambers. He later admitted that he might have known Chambers after all—but by a different name. Chambers testified that Hiss had given him dozens of top-secret documents for delivery to a Russian spy. In early December, Chambers led investigators to a garden behind his house, reached into a hollowed-out pumpkin, and pulled out rolls of microfilm of the documents that he said Hiss had stolen. Some of the so-called "Pumpkin Papers" were in Hiss's handwriting, and others were typed on his typewriter. On December 15, 1948, Hiss was indicted on two counts of *perjury* (lying under oath). Later, a jury found Hiss guilty. He served 44 months in prison.

Nixon studies microfilm of government documents supplied by Whittaker Chambers in the investigation of accused spy Alger Hiss. The investigation brought Nixon to national attention in 1948.

The Hiss case made Nixon a national figure and a hero to staunch anti-Communists. Alger Hiss spent the rest of his life trying to clear himself of the charges, denying that he was ever a Soviet spy. People disagree on his guilt or innocence to this day.

In the meantime, the Nixons had other reasons to be happy that year. Their second daughter, Julie, was born in July 1948. In November Nixon easily won a second term in Congress.

Moving Up ———————————————————

In 1950, during his third two-year term in the House, Nixon began a run for a U.S. Senate seat. His opponent was Democrat Helen Gahagan Douglas, a former actress and the wife of a leading Hollywood movie star. A popular and glamorous figure, Douglas had also served three terms in the House. Nixon did not try to become glamorous. Instead, he portrayed himself as the all-American family man. He and Pat drove around California in a wood-paneled station wagon. At each stop, Pat handed out thimbles stamped "Nixon for Senate."

Once again, Nixon went on the attack, suggesting that Douglas had ties with Communism. People called Communists "Reds" and those who supported them "Pinks." Nixon's campaign printed up thousands of "Pink Sheets," handouts that distorted Douglas's voting record to make her appear sympathetic to Communist causes. He accused Douglas of being "pink right down to her under-wear." The Douglas campaign responded with attacks of its own. Douglas herself gave Nixon a nickname that would shadow him for the rest of his life—"Tricky

A poster for Nixon in his victorious run for the U.S. Senate against Democrat Helen Gahagan Douglas.

Dick." On election day, however, Nixon won by the largest margin of any senator that year.

"We hopped from one victory celebration to another far into the night," Pat recalled. "Dick was so exuberant. Wherever he found a piano he played 'Happy Days Are Here Again.'" It was an appropriate song. At age 38, Nixon was about to become the youngest member of the U.S. Senate, and even bigger accomplishments lay ahead.

Chapter 3

Running Mates

On July 11, 1952, Dick and Pat Nixon were in Chicago for the Republican National Convention. Earlier, the party had nominated Dwight D. Eisenhower, the popular World War II general, to run for president. Now Pat Nixon was having lunch with a friend at a Chicago restaurant. Just as she took the first bite of her sandwich, the restaurant's television flashed a news bulletin: General Eisenhower had chosen Richard Nixon to be his vice presidential candidate. "That bite of sandwich popped right out of my mouth," Pat recalled.

Pat thought that Nixon would turn down a vice presidential nomination, but clearly he had accepted it. She rushed to the convention hall, arriving in time to stand with her husband onstage while the crowd cheered and whooped their congratulations. Pat had never liked campaigning, and had hoped that Dick would return to law

After Nixon's nomination to run for vice president, Pat and Richard Nixon wave to the convention crowd with presidential nominee Dwight Eisenhower and his wife Mamie.

practice and a more normal family life, yet she respected his decision and would campaign energetically.

Known to all as "Ike," Dwight Eisenhower was a mild, grandfatherly man who inspired trust and admiration. By contrast, Nixon was young and energetic. He had made many friends in the Republican party and was known as an effective campaigner. Eisenhower assigned Nixon to deliver Republican attacks on the Democratic candidates. Before long, however, Nixon was under attack himself.

The Checkers Speech

In September 1952, just as Nixon began a campaign tour of the West Coast, the *New York Post* ran a sensational front-page story under the headline: "SECRET NIXON FUND." It reported that Nixon had a special fund of $18,000 contributed by millionaire Republicans and accused Nixon of using the money for personal expenses.

Nixon admitted that the fund existed, but denied that he had misused the money. His campaign treasurer released evidence that many contributors to the fund were not millionaires but small businessmen and that Nixon had used the money only for campaign expenses. Still, the accusations cut deeply, raising old questions about Nixon's ethics. Many leading Republicans urged Nixon to resign from the ticket. Even Eisenhower had doubts.

Nixon was determined to stay on the ticket. He demanded a chance to defend himself publicly, and the Republican campaign arranged a half-hour of television time on the major networks. Minutes before the broadcast, Nixon was nervous. "I just don't think I can go through with this one," he said to Pat.

"Of course you can," she said. She took his hand and walked him into the broadcast studio.

Nixon spoke to 60 million viewers, then the largest television audience in history. Calmly, he explained he had not spent one penny of the contributions for personal use. He listed the family's finances item by item. "It isn't very much, but Pat and I have the satisfaction that every dime we've got is honestly ours." Finally, Nixon made a winning admission. They had kept one gift, he said, a black-and-white cocker spaniel named Checkers. "And you know, the kids love that dog and I just want to say this right now, that regardless of what they say about it, we're going to keep it."

Nixon asked viewers to send telegrams to the Republican National Committee supporting or opposing him. "Whatever their decision is," he said, "I will abide by it." Some 4 million messages poured in, and a large majority urged Nixon to stay on. The Republican National Committee voted to keep him on the ticket. Soon afterward, Nixon arrived in West Virginia to campaign with Eisenhower. Ike met him with a grin and the welcome words, "You're my boy."

In his televised "Checkers" speech, Nixon defends himself against charges that he had used secret campaign contributions for personal expenses.

Nixon's critics were less impressed by the "Checkers" speech. They claimed that he hadn't really answered charges about the fund and its contributors, and they criticized him for appealing to listeners by drawing a sentimental portrait of his family.

Vice President

In November, voters elected Eisenhower and Nixon in a landslide over the Democratic candidates, Adlai Stevenson and John Sparkman. The Republican ticket received more than 55 percent of the popular vote, and 442 votes in the electoral college to Stevenson's 89.

Ike had promised that he would assign important tasks to Nixon during his term of office, and Nixon soon became one of the busiest and most active vice presidents up to that time. He made goodwill visits to many nations of the world and became a serious student of U.S. foreign policy. Foreign affairs remained his greatest interest and later become a focus of his own presidency.

Nixon also devoted attention to Republican politics. Eisenhower, who had never served in elective office or participated in party politics, was a Republican outsider. Nixon was a party insider. He raised funds for the party and campaigned for dozens of Republican candidates. In addition, he carried on a constant battle with Democratic leaders about their policies. Democrats came to despise Nixon. *Washington Post* cartoonist Herblock defined Nixon's sinister side, exaggerating his ski-jump nose, fleshy jowls, and heavy "five-o'clock shadow."

On September 24, 1955, Nixon learned that Eisenhower had suffered a heart attack. Although Eisenhower never transferred his duties officially to

Nixon, the vice president took on additional responsibilities and handled the new situation with tact and dignity. Within six weeks, Eisenhower returned to the White House. In February 1956, he announced he would run for a second term. That summer Eisenhower and Nixon easily won the Republican nominations. Once again, the Democrats nominated Adlai Stevenson for president.

In the campaign, Democrats focused their attacks on Richard Nixon. They played on the possibility Eisenhower could die in office. One advertisement asked, "Nervous about Nixon?

President Dwight D. Eisenhower, under whom Nixon served as vice president for eight years.

President Nixon?" Nixon did not reply. In this campaign he concentrated on the accomplishments of the Eisenhower administration and refused to go on the attack. People spoke of a "new Nixon." On election night 1956, Eisenhower and Nixon were easily re-elected.

A Traveling Man

In the spring of 1958, Nixon embarked with Pat on a goodwill trip to South America. The early stops went well, but in Lima, Peru, demonstrators angry about the "imperialist" policies of the United States, hurled rocks, bottles, and oranges at Nixon. Soon afterward, at the airport in Caracas, Venezuela, anti-American demonstrators spat tobacco juice on Pat and Dick. As the Nixon motorcade left the airport, hundreds of angry demonstrators wielding clubs, pipes, and rocks surrounded Nixon's car. The driver couldn't get through the thick crowd. Shouting insults, the mob began to rock the car, trying to turn it over. Finally, Venezuelan soldiers were able to clear a path through the human roadblock.

Photographs of the angry scene filled front pages in the United States. Reporters praised the vice president's brave conduct. When the Nixons arrived back in Washington D.C., President Eisenhower and a crowd of more than 15,000 greeted them at the airport. They were hailed as heroes.

A trip to Moscow in 1959 once again put Nixon in the international spotlight. As Nixon toured a U.S. exhibition featuring a model kitchen with Soviet premier Nikita Khrushchev, the two leaders began to debate the advantages of Communism and democracy. Nixon tactfully answered Khrushchev's hostile questions. He stressed the advantages of the personal freedom and the need for

In 1958 an angry crowd in Caracas, Venezuela, attacks the car Nixon is riding in, protesting U.S. policies in Latin America.

Nixon and Soviet premier Nikita Khrushchev carry on a lively debate during Nixon's visit to Moscow in 1959. Nixon defended U.S. freedoms and economic policies.

peace in the world. A recording of the "kitchen debate" appeared on U.S. television, and Nixon received widespread praise for standing up to Khrushchev and emphasizing peace.

A New Frontier

As the 1960 presidential election approached, Richard Nixon announced his candidacy for president. He easily won the Republican nomination, then took personal control of his campaign. He approved slogans on bumper stickers, chose his campaign stops, and directed overall strategy. He worked at a breakneck pace, even pledging to visit all 50 states (Alaska and Hawaii had become states in 1959).

Campaign pins for Nixon and Kennedy in the 1960 presidential race.

His opponent was John F. Kennedy, a handsome young Democrat from Massachusetts. Kennedy came from a background starkly different from Nixon's. Both of his grandfathers had been leading politicians, and his father was a wealthy investment banker and a power in Democratic politics. Kennedy had attended the finest prep schools and graduated from Harvard. Self-assured and at ease with himself, Kennedy offered a contrast to Nixon, who often seemed self-conscious and awkward.

Nixon had to walk a tricky line in his campaign. As the current vice president, he had to endorse the policies of the Eisenhower administration, but he also needed to show how his presidency would be different. He came up with a clever line, "A record is never something to stand on. It's something to build on." Kennedy described "A New Frontier," pledging to improve the economy and "get America moving again."

When Kennedy challenged Nixon to the first nationally televised debates between presidential candidates, Nixon's advisers warned him not to accept. Nixon was much better known than Kennedy, and debates would only give the Democratic candidate exposure. Still, Nixon could not resist a debate, and he agreed to meet Kennedy four times.

In the weeks before the first debate, Nixon injured his knee, which became infected and sent him to the hospital for a two-week stay. Once out of the hospital, he caught the flu, but continued to campaign despite fever and chills. When he arrived for the first debate, on September 26, 1960, Nixon had lost so much weight that his shirt collar hung loose. On camera, he looked pale, and sweat dampened his face as he spoke. On the other side of the stage, Kennedy looked tan, handsome, and relaxed.

Eighty million television viewers tuned in to the first debate—the largest television audience since Nixon's "Checkers" speech. Most viewers concluded that Kennedy won the debate. His winning manner and easy charm gave him a huge boost in the opinion polls. For the first time, a candidate's appearance and on-camera manner played a major role in a presidential election. For the other

Kennedy (left) and Nixon (right) before the first-ever televised debate between presidential candidates. Kennedy's healthy good looks and self-assured manner gave him an advantage against Nixon, who looked pale and ill at ease.

three debates Nixon looked and performed better on camera, but he never regained the advantage he lost in the first debate.

On election day, the vote was extremely close, with each candidate getting roughly half the votes. Out of 68 million votes cast, Kennedy had only 113,000 more than Nixon. In the electoral college, Kennedy gained 303 votes to Nixon's 219, but even here, the shift of a few thousand votes in a few large states could have changed the outcome. Republicans charged that vote-counting frauds in Texas and Illinois may have made the difference. President Eisenhower urged Nixon to demand a recount, but he refused, arguing that a recount would cause political chaos. John F. Kennedy became the youngest person ever elected to the presidency. For Nixon, it was an agonizing defeat.

The "Last" Press Conference

The Nixons returned to California, where Dick joined a large Los Angeles law firm. After 24 years in Washington, however, Nixon found legal practice dull. Then in 1962, California Republicans asked him to run for governor. He ran an energetic campaign, but it sometimes seemed his heart was not truly in it. Once again, he accused his opponent, Democratic governor Edmund "Pat" Brown, of being soft on Communism. This time, the tactic didn't work. Nixon lost the election by 297,000 votes.

The Nixon family in California during Nixon's campaign for governor. Later, both Tricia (seated at left) and Julie (at right) were married while their father was president.

In a press conference the next morning, Nixon congratulated Governor Brown. Then he lashed out at the press, accusing them of giving him unfair coverage during the campaign—and ever since the Hiss case, 14 years earlier. "Just think how much you're going to be missing," he said. "You won't have Nixon to kick around anymore, because, gentlemen, this is my last conference."

This angry outburst seemed to destroy any hope Nixon had for future political success. The following week, *Time Magazine* declared, "Barring a miracle, his political career ended last week." Nixon still had a wide and sympathetic following, however. He received thousands of letters of approval for his outburst. Many Republicans agreed that the press was against them, and they were proud that Nixon had dared to say so.

Nixon himself never believed that his loss to Pat Brown or his anger with reporters had finished his political career. Before long, he began plotting his comeback.

Chapter 4

"No Other Life for Me"

In 1963 the Nixons moved from California to New York City, where Nixon joined a prominent and politically connected law firm. His work included frequent trips abroad, and he soon proved his worth to the firm, becoming a senior partner.

In the meantime, the political scene was changing rapidly. Later that year President John F. Kennedy was shot and killed by an assassin while on a visit to Dallas, Texas. His vice president, Lyndon B. Johnson, was sworn in to complete his term. The following year, Johnson ran for a full term as president against conservative Republican candidate Barry Goldwater. Nixon had stayed out of the race for the Republican nomination, but after Goldwater's nomination, Nixon reappeared to travel the country, campaigning for Republican candidates.

Nixon later wrote that he had been discontented out of politics. "I had finally come to realize that there was no other life for me but politics and public service," he said. Barry Goldwater lost the 1964 election by a landslide vote to President Johnson, but Nixon made many new friends with his support for the party. In fact, the campaign proved to be the first step of his political comeback.

Trying Times

Johnson's term proved to be one of the most difficult and tempestuous in recent history. Overseas, the United States was becoming more involved in the war in Vietnam. Communist fighters called the Vietcong were trying to overthrow the government of South Vietnam, an American ally. President Kennedy had sent military advisers. Now Johnson was sending thousands of U.S. troops to avoid a Communist takeover. At the same time, the Communist government of North Vietnam began to provide increasing aid to the Vietcong. By 1968, there were more than 500,000 U.S. troops in Vietnam, but the stubborn Vietnamese guerrillas continued to fight.

At home, African Americans rioted in one city after another, protesting mistreatment by largely white police forces, discrimination in housing, and other grievances. Riots in Watts (a section of Los Angeles), Detroit, and Newark resulted in hundreds of deaths and injuries and millions of dollars in property damage.

Things were changing in American homes as well. Teenagers began sporting long hair, experimenting with drugs, and listening to music their parents considered objectionable and dangerous. Increasingly, students took part in political demonstrations favoring civil rights and opposing the growing war in Vietnam. Rebellious young people seemed to be questioning all authority.

1968

On February 2, 1968, Richard Nixon announced that he would seek the Republican nomination for president. That same day, North Vietnamese and Vietcong fighters began a major new offensive in South Vietnam. They attacked more than 100 South Vietnamese cities and reached the outskirts of Saigon, the South Vietnamese capital. U.S. troops managed to beat back the attacks, but the devastating offensive persuaded many Americans that U.S. victory in Vietnam was impossible. A new wave of antiwar protests swept the nation.

On March 30, Lyndon Johnson surprised the nation in a televised address, announcing that he would not run for a second term as president. Harried by antiwar protestors and facing an antiwar revolt in his own party, he chose to use the last days of his term to seek an end to the war. In early April, civil rights leader Martin Luther King Jr. was assassinated in Memphis, Tennessee, where he was organizing a Poor Peoples' March. That night, further riots engulfed several

1968 was a tumultuous year. At left, Vietcong troops shell the South Vietnamese capital during a major offensive in January. Right, President Lyndon Johnson announces he will not run for re-election in April. Below, antiwar protesters clash with police during the Democratic convention in Chicago in August, overshadowing the nomination of Hubert Humphrey to run against Nixon. In November, Nixon was elected president.

major cities. On June 5, Senator Robert Kennedy, the brother of the slain president, was assassinated in Los Angeles only hours after winning the California Democratic presidential primary. It seemed to many Americans that the country was falling apart.

In August, Richard Nixon came to the Republican National Convention as the party's leading presidential candidate. Holding the middle ground between liberal Nelson Rockefeller and conservative Ronald Reagan, Nixon won nomination on the first ballot.

Later that month, the Democratic convention in Chicago faced thousands of demonstrators against President Johnson and the war. When demonstrators taunted the police, the police attacked, causing a long night of disorder in which many were injured and many others arrested. Inside the convention hall, Vice President Hubert Humphrey, who supported President Johnson's war policies, was nominated for president.

In Alabama, former governor George Wallace helped organize the American Independent party and became its presidential candidate. Wallace defended the old southern racial policies of *segregation* (legal separation of African Americans) and campaigned against federal government actions to end those policies. He gained a broad following in the Deep South.

The Campaign

The nation had not been so deeply divided since the Civil War. Richard Nixon campaigned on three themes. First, he pledged to "bring us together." Second, he called for "peace with honor" in Vietnam. He pledged to end the war and to bring American soldiers home. Finally, he supported a "return to law and order," deploring the urban riots and growing antiwar demonstrations.

The Nixon campaign was carefully organized. This time, Nixon conserved his energy, giving fewer speeches and choosing their sites carefully. Instead of debates, he relied on televised "town meetings," in which he answered questions from small, friendly audiences. Outside the television studio, campaigning was difficult. Each of the three candidates was met at every appearance by demonstrators and hecklers.

On election night, Nixon sat by himself in a suite at the Waldorf-Astoria Towers hotel in New York City, following the returns. The race was very close, but late that evening it was clear that Nixon had been elected. He left his solitary observation post and celebrated with his family in a nearby suite. After stinging defeats in 1960 and 1962, Richard Nixon would become the 37th president of the United States. He received 43.4 percent of the vote to Humphrey's 42.7 percent. In the electoral college, Nixon had 301 votes, Humphrey 191, and Wallace 46.

The next day, a grinning Nixon spoke to supporters. "Having lost a close one eight years ago and having won a close one this year, I can say this—winning's a lot more fun."

Nixon and his family celebrate on election night, after he defeats Hubert Humphrey and gains the presidency.

A few weeks later, the Nixons celebrated another happy occasion. Their daughter Julie married David Eisenhower, a grandson of former president Eisenhower. The uniting of these two political families captivated the American public and the press.

Getting Started

Inauguration day, January 20, 1969, arrived gray and dreary with a cutting wind. Pat Nixon held the two Milhous family Bibles while her husband took the oath of office. Then President Nixon spoke. His inaugural address focused on his commitment to secure peace. "The greatest honor history can bestow is the title of peacemaker," he said. "This honor now beckons America."

The ride down Pennsylvania Avenue to the White House showed just how difficult that role would be. Hundreds of demonstrators threw sticks, stones, and beer cans at the president's limousine. They burned small American flags and traded insults with Republican spectators. It was the first time in history that an inaugural parade had been disrupted.

Nixon's team was already in place. He had carefully selected his cabinet and top staff. Unlike most politicians, Nixon did not want to talk to many people. A shy and self-conscious man, he preferred memos to meetings. He relied heavily on a few top aides, who would filter everyone else's messages to the president.

One man Nixon did see regularly was Henry Kissinger, his national security adviser. The two worked closely on foreign policy, especially on negotiations to end the war in Vietnam. Soon after Nixon's election, Kissinger began secret peace talks in addition to the official negotiations begun by Lyndon Johnson. Ending the war in Vietnam was the administration's main priority. It dominated much of Nixon's first term in office.

President Nixon confers with his national security adviser, Henry Kissinger, during a flight on *Air Force One*.

Nixon was obsessed by what the press said about him, yet he considered them "the enemy." He started each day reading the "News Summary," a selection of comments from television, newspapers, and magazines prepared by his staff. Nixon scrawled notes in the margins, giving instructions to his assistants. Often he lashed out at reporters who criticized the administration, writing such comments as "freeze him," "dump him," and "knock this down." The staff kept a "freeze list" of people who would not be invited to White House functions. It later grew into the administration's "enemies list," which would be disclosed in court in 1974 during the Watergate crisis.

☆ ☆ ☆

Vietnam

When Nixon took office, 550,000 American troops were serving in Vietnam. As the war dragged on and casualties increased, many Americans couldn't understand why the United States was involved in this war. They argued that a Communist government in Vietnam didn't threaten Americans. Others disagreed. They said it was essential for the United States to help fight the spread of Communism anywhere.

In the spring of 1969, Nixon announced his plan for "Vietnamization." The United States, he said, would train and arm South Vietnamese soldiers to replace American troops. As the South Vietnamese became better able to fight the war themselves, American soldiers would gradually return home. In June he announced the withdrawal of the first 25,000 troops.

In a nationally televised speech on November 3, 1969, Nixon appealed for support for his war aims. He was tired of the "vocal minority" that protested and demonstrated. He asked the "great silent majority" of Americans for their support. Phone calls and telegrams were overwhelmingly in favor of Nixon, but they didn't stop the protests.

Meanwhile, Nixon ordered the secret bombing of Cambodia and Laos, countries that bordered Vietnam. These countries were *neutral*, supporting neither side in the war, but Communist forces were using their territory to store supplies. Nixon hoped the bombing would cut off supplies and reduce the effectiveness of enemy forces. On April 30, 1970, Nixon ordered a ground invasion of Cambodia to clear out Communist weapon stockpiles.

The invasion succeeded, but it killed scores of innocent civilians and brought a firestorm of protest at home. It seemed that Nixon was expanding the war rather than ending it. As protesters gathered on college campuses, some states called out National Guard troops to keep order. At Kent State University in Ohio, inexperienced guardsmen fired into a crowd of demonstrators. Four

A student at Kent State University in Ohio lies dead after National Guard troops fired into a group of antiwar protesters in April 1970. They were protesting President Nixon's attack on the neutral nation of Cambodia.

students were killed and others were wounded. Protests on other campuses grew. Many colleges closed early that spring in order to avoid violence.

By mid-1971, nearly half of the American troops had been withdrawn from Vietnam. Then in March 1972, North Vietnamese forces launched their biggest offensive yet. Nixon ordered an all-out counterattack, with heavy bombing. Hopes for peace dimmed yet again. Meanwhile, Henry Kissinger worked diligently to arrive at a peace settlement in talks with the North Vietnamese in Paris.

As Nixon's run for re-election approached in 1972, he was eager to conclude a peace settlement. Henry Kissinger and Vietnamese representatives had nearly completed an agreement. Late in October, however, America's ally, the South Vietnamese government, refused to sign. Kissinger announced "peace is at hand," but he could not produce a signed agreement.

After the election, in mid-December 1972, Nixon and Kissinger made one more show of force to compel the North Vietnamese to end the fighting. For twelve days, American B-52 bombers attacked the North Vietnamese cities of Hanoi and Haiphong. Americans were outraged at what appeared to be another expansion of the war. The *New York Times* called the bombings "stone-age barbarism." Nixon defended his decision, later writing that it was the most difficult decision he made during the war but "also one of the most clear-cut and necessary ones."

Shortly after the bombings, both sides returned to the peace talks and finally arrived at an agreement. The Paris Peace Accords were signed, and a cease-fire went into effect on January 27, 1973. Americans rejoiced that their involvement in the brutal war was finally over. The cost of the war had been devastating. Some 58,000 Americans died and more than 300,000 were wounded. Vietnamese losses were much higher, including nearly a million fighters on both sides and uncounted civilian deaths during battles and bombings. Opponents of the war asked why a similar agreement was not signed years earlier.

Steps, Far and Near ——

Even as war and controversy raged, other momentous achievements were unfolding. On July 20, 1969, the United States landed men on the moon for the first time. Millions watched on television as

---

Fast Facts

THE VIETNAM WAR

Who: Communist guerrilla fighters in South Vietnam (the Vietcong) and military units from Communist North Vietnam against South Vietnamese and United States troops

When: 1958–1975

Why: Vietnam was temporarily divided in Northern (Communist) and Southern (non-Communist) zones in 1954; when elections were not held in the South in 1956, Communist guerrillas began to attack the government. The U.S. first sent military advisers, then large numbers of combatants to support South Vietnam; North Vietnam entered the war in support of the Vietcong.

Where: North and South Vietnam, and border regions of Cambodia and Laos

Outcome: U.S. troops were withdrawn after a 1973 cease-fire, but fighting resumed between Communist and non-Communist forces. In 1975, Communist forces took possession of the South, dissolved the government, and unified Vietnam under a Communist government.

President Nixon phoned the astronauts Neil Armstrong and Buzz Aldrin on the moon. "This certainly has to be the most historic phone call ever made from the White House," he said.

White House Wedding

On June 12, 1971, the Nixons took part in a historic family event. Their daughter Tricia married Edward Cox, a law student, in the Rose Garden of the White House. It was the first wedding ever held in the Rose Garden. "It was a day that all of us will remember because we were beautifully and simply happy," Nixon later wrote.

President Nixon escorts his daughter Tricia to her wedding ceremony in the Rose Garden at the White House in June 1971.

☆★☆

Nixon also began many important new government initiatives. In partnership with Congress, he helped establish the Environmental Protection Agency and pass a new Clean Air Act. "Clean air, clean water, open spaces—these should be the birthright of every American," Nixon declared. He also established the Occupational Safety and Health Administration to ensure safe working environments for Americans, and the Endangered Species Act to help save animals in danger of extinction. Under Nixon, the voting age changed from 21 to 18, and drafting of Americans into military service ended.

World Leader

Although his administration devoted untold hours to the war in Vietnam, Richard Nixon became most famous for his other foreign policy initiatives. In February 1972 he surprised the world by making an official visit to Mainland China. Ever since a Communist government had taken over China in 1949, the United States had refused to recognize the most populous country on Earth. Now, 23 years later, Nixon met with Chinese leaders, including Chairman Mao Zedong. Richard and Pat Nixon charmed their hosts, and their sightseeing visits to the Great Wall of China and other landmarks captivated people around the world. The visit was also a diplomatic success, beginning a process that

Nixon reviews troops during his historic visit to the People's Republic of China in 1972. Chinese leader Zhou Enlai is at left center, and Pat Nixon is at center.

established full diplomatic relations with China six years later. The "opening" to China would be hailed as one of Nixon's finest achievements.

Several months later, President Nixon and Pat flew to Moscow. There the president met with Soviet premier Leonid Brezhnev. Since 1969, the Nixon administration had been in talks with the Soviet Union about limiting the manufacture of nuclear weapons. Now, in June 1972, Nixon and Brezhnev signed the Strategic Arms Limitation Treaty, or SALT, marking a turning point in relations between the United States and the Soviet Union. It was a significant step toward arms control.

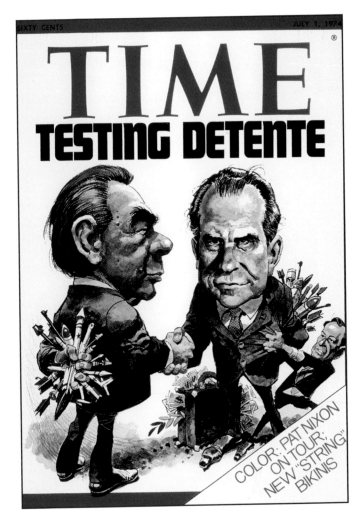

A *Time Magazine* cover shows Soviet premier Leonid Brezhnev and President Nixon shaking hands on an arms limitation treaty while hiding weapons behind their backs.

Contradictions

Nixon was accomplishing historic triumphs abroad and progressive achievements at home. But within the White House, close aides saw a different Nixon—he had turned into an angry, suspicious man. In early 1971, Nixon set up an elaborate voice-activated tape-recording system in his offices. He believed the tapes would help him write his memoirs, but he also knew that the recorded comments of unfriendly visitors might someday be used against them. He was not the first president to set up secret recording devices, but his system was far more extensive than those used by Presidents Kennedy and Johnson.

Nixon's fears and suspicions were heightened in June 1971, when the *New York Times* and other newspapers began publishing the "Pentagon Papers," a secret government report on the history of U.S. involvement in Vietnam. Daniel Ellsberg, a Pentagon researcher who helped prepare the report, "leaked" copies of it to reporters.

The papers contained nothing about Nixon or his administration. Still, Nixon and Henry Kissinger believed that publishing the papers was a threat to national security. They would reveal earlier secret negotiations and make future negotiations more difficult. The administration took legal action against the newspapers, seeking to stop further publication, but the courts ruled in favor of press freedom.

More ominously, Nixon ordered that a team be assembled to stop further leaks in the government. This secret group called themselves the "plumbers," since their main job was plugging leaks. They also took on other special projects. One of these was to find damaging information about Daniel Ellsberg so that the administration could embarrass him publicly. Two of the plumbers, G. Gordon Liddy and Howard Hunt, broke into Ellsberg's psychiatrist's office in California, hoping to find damaging information about Ellsberg's mental health. They didn't find anything, but they escaped undetected. Later, their lawless escapade was discovered by government investigators and became part of the Watergate scandal.

In January 1972, Nixon and his supporters set up the Committee to Re-Elect the President (CRP), to run his campaign in the fall. Former plumber Liddy went to work for the committee. In early June, when Nixon was toasting Brezhnev at the Kremlin, Liddy and Hunt attempted another illegal venture. They supervised a break-in at the offices of the Democratic National Committee (DNC) in the Watergate, a luxury apartment–office development in Washington, to place recording "bugs" on the phones of DNC director Larry O'Brien, who was at the top of the White House enemies list. They soon learned that the bugs had failed.

In the early morning of June 17, 1972, the Hunt and Liddy group broke into the DNC again. This time, the results would set off a chain of events that brought the downfall of President Richard Nixon.

Chapter 5

Caught

At two o'clock in the morning on June 17, 1972, a guard discovered an unusual situation at the Watergate complex in Washington, D.C. Someone had taped a door so that it would not lock. Soon afterward, police arrived and discovered five men in the office of the Democratic National Committee. They didn't look like run-of-the-mill burglars. They were dressed in suits and ties and were carrying cameras, electronic listening equipment, and 53 crisp $100 bills.

Investigators soon connected the five burglars to the Committee to Re-Elect the President. One of the men was CRP's chief of security. Another carried an address book that contained a phone number for Howard Hunt's office in the White House. Investigators soon arrested Hunt and his partner Gordon Liddy, who had masterminded the break-in. Despite the connection, the story got little notice at first.

Nixon learned of the break-in at a friend's home in the Bahamas, where he was on a short vacation. According to Nixon, he first thought the break-in was a foolish prank, but later evidence suggests he may have known about the plans ahead of time. What is clear is that within days, President Nixon decided to end the investigations of the break-in.

Why would Nixon have bothered to cover up this small incident? Other presidents may have bugged their opponents during campaigns. Even though it was wrong, it might not be disastrous. Nixon knew, however, that a thorough investigation of the break-in would lead to the discovery of other illegal activities in which the president's men had been involved, such as the break-in at Ellsberg's psychiatrist's office. On June 19, the president issued a public statement about Watergate: "There was no involvement whatever by White House personnel."

Tape recordings from Nixon's offices, revealed during the investigation, tell a different story. The president and his top aides began discussing how to maintain the cover-up. In a conversation on June 23, Nixon agreed to a plan to order the FBI to end its investigation of Watergate by claiming that national security secrets were involved. Two years later, this "smoking gun" tape was the final piece of evidence that broke the president. It showed conclusively that Nixon been trying to end the investigation from the beginning.

Landslide ———————————————————

At first, it seemed that the Watergate break-in would fade away. Through the summer, most attention was on the presidential campaign. In July, the Democrats nominated Senator George McGovern, a liberal Democrat deeply opposed to the Vietnam War. Nixon was confident that McGovern was far too liberal to defeat him. At campaign rallies, Nixon spoke about his "new American revolution." He wanted to streamline the bulky federal government, reducing it in size and scope. In foreign policy he talked about continuing détente, or easing of tensions, with the Soviet Union and other Communist governments. Cheering crowds yelled, "Nixon, Now More than Ever."

In November, Nixon spent election night in the Lincoln Sitting Room, his favorite spot in the White House. Soon it became apparent that he would win by a landslide. He received 60.7 percent of the popular vote and won every state except Massachusetts. Despite this, Nixon was melancholy that night. Instead of enjoying the victory, he was brooding about the stalling Vietnam peace talks. Finally, ten weeks later, he was able to announce a cease-fire in Vietnam.

Spotlight ———————————————————

Meanwhile, public interest in Watergate was growing. In January 1973, Hunt, Liddy, and the five Watergate burglars were found guilty. The trial judge, though, did not feel satisfied that the full story had been uncovered. Soon afterward, one of the convicted men wrote a letter to the judge, claiming that the burglars were pressured to plead guilty and that some witnesses had lied. Meanwhile, the Senate voted to set up a special committee to investigate Watergate. Gradually the committee's investigators uncovered details of the case. The cast of characters was large, and the plot was complicated, involving "hush money" paid to the burglars to encourage their silence, and bribes, threats, and lies. Day after day, the trail led investigators higher and higher within the White House.

By April the investigation had cast suspicion on Nixon's two senior advisers in the White House. In addition, John Dean, the president's *counsel* (legal adviser), was cooperating with investigators. Nixon decided he had to separate himself from everyone implicated in the scandal. On April 30, he accepted the resignations of his two top advisers and fired John Dean. Yet he professed to support further investigation and denied his own involvement.

On May 24, Nixon threw a huge party at the White House for the nearly 600 prisoners of war recently returned from Vietnam. Three weeks later, Soviet president Leonid Brezhnev visited Washington. In a formal ceremony at the White House, Nixon and Brezhnev signed the historic Prevention of Nuclear War Treaty. It committed the countries with nuclear weapons to consult with each other before using them.

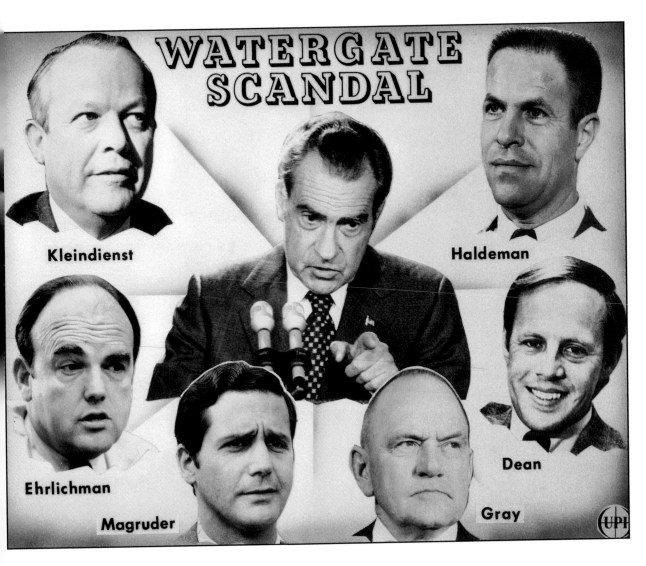

Nixon with six members of his administration who had resigned or been fired in the Watergate scandal by May 1973. They include Attorney General Richard Kleindienst, top White House advisers Bob Haldeman and John Ehrlichman, special White House assistant Jeb Magruder, acting FBI director L. Patrick Gray, and counsel to the president John Dean.

The country's interest that summer was focused on Watergate, however. On May 17, the Senate Watergate Committee began televised hearings. In June, millions watched in fascination as the president's former legal counsel, John Dean, took the stand. In a long prepared statement, Dean made shocking charges. He directly accused the president of participating in the cover-up, but he had no actual evidence—it was his word against the president's. That was soon to change. On July 16, a White House aide named Alexander Butterfield told the committee about Nixon's tape-recording system. This was the turning point of the Watergate investigation. The tapes would show who was telling the truth, Dean or Nixon.

The Senate committee immediately requested from Nixon all tapes and documents associated with Watergate. Nixon refused to hand over the tapes, claiming *executive privilege*, the president's right to have confidential conversations with his aides and advisers. He said there were "a great many very frank and very private comments" on subjects that had nothing to do with Watergate. The release of the conversations could harm the government.

Congress also forced Nixon to appoint a special prosecutor to make a criminal investigation of Watergate matters. Reluctantly, Nixon appointed Archibald Cox, a distinguished former judge and law professor. Cox issued a *subpoena*, a legal demand, for seven of the White House tapes. The president offered to compromise by providing written summaries of the tapes. In October, Cox refused the compromise. Nixon angrily ordered his attorney general to fire Cox. The attorney general refused, and resigned instead. Nixon ordered the deputy attorney general to fire Cox. When he refused, Nixon fired him. Finally, the third highest official in the department followed Nixon's orders and fired Cox.

The episode, known as the Saturday Night Massacre, caused an enormous uproar. Hundreds of thousands of citizens called, wrote, and telegraphed their representatives in Washington, demanding action against Nixon. He had not broken a law by firing Cox, but his willingness to fire the special prosecutor and other high-ranking legal officials made him appear to be guilty. His approval rating dropped to 17 percent in a Gallup poll. People started to call for Nixon's *impeachment*, a process of accusation and trial that could remove him from office. Shaken, Nixon agreed to turn over the seven tapes.

"I Am Not a Crook"

Meanwhile, scandal claimed another Nixon man. Early in October, Vice President Spiro Agnew was formally charged with bribery and tax evasion when he served as governor of Maryland. Rather than go to trial, Agnew agreed to resign as vice president. Nixon nominated Representative Gerald Ford to be the new vice president, and Ford was soon confirmed by Congress.

The president's personal finances were also under scrutiny. He was accused of not paying proper income taxes and of using campaign funds to help pay for his house in California. At a press conference in November, a reporter asked Nixon about his tax problems. Nixon, sweat glistening on his forehead, leaned forward and said, "I welcome this kind of examination because people have got to know whether or not their President is a crook. Well, I am not a crook. I have earned everything I have got." In the end, Nixon was ordered to pay $500,000 in back taxes.

The Senate committee issued a subpoena for hundreds of additional tapes. Nixon refused. One court after another ordered him to surrender the tapes. Finally, the case was heard by the U.S. Supreme Court. While the court was considering the case, Nixon made one further effort to gain credit for openness. He released edited transcripts of the subpoenaed tapes. In a televised speech from the Oval Office on April 29, 1974, he displayed a stack of blue folders, which contained edited transcriptions of all the requested tapes. His secretaries had removed any swear words, replacing them with the words "expletive deleted."

The committee refused to accept the transcripts and still demanded the actual tapes. Even worse, the transcripts were soon published and became a best seller, as a fascinated public learned how ugly and hostile many of the Nixon conversations were. The *Chicago Tribune* wrote, "We have seen the private man and

Investigators in the special prosecutor's office, the Senate Watergate Committee, and the House Judiciary Committee spent endless hours listening to the White House tapes on equipment like this.

we are appalled." The phrase "expletive deleted," which appeared often on nearly every page, became a running joke.

On May 9, 1974, the House Judiciary Committee opened hearings to decide whether to recommend the impeachment of President Richard Nixon. It was only the second time in history that Congress had begun impeachment proceedings against a president.

While the Watergate scandal approached its climax, Nixon made one last diplomatic journey, visiting the Middle East, where another war had occurred months earlier. This "journey of peace" was a huge boost for Nixon's morale. He remained popular and respected in most countries of the world, even as he lost his following at home. In Egypt, Nixon was greeted by more than a million cheering supporters.

Dire Decision

On July 24, 1974, the Supreme Court unanimously ordered Nixon to turn over the subpoenaed tapes. Executive privilege, the court said, did not apply to cases involving possible criminal behavior. Nixon could argue no more. He turned over the tapes, knowing that one of them contained the smoking gun that proved that he had been lying to the public and to Congress for two years.

Even before the new tapes were made public, the House Judiciary Committee voted to bring three articles of impeachment against Nixon. These articles were like indictments in a criminal trial. If the articles were approved by the full House, its leaders would act as prosecutors in a trial of the president, and the Senate would sit as a jury. If the Senate voted Nixon guilty on any article by a two-thirds majority, he would be convicted and removed from office.

Knowing that the game was nearly up, Nixon made one final attempt to gain public support. He released the transcript of the smoking gun tape of June 23, 1972, to the public with a note claiming that he did not believe the contents justified "the extreme step of impeachment and removal of a president." The public reaction was immediate and devastating. Citizens, members of Congress, and leading Republicans felt betrayed and outraged when they learned that Nixon had been lying to them for two long years. Republicans who had stood behind Nixon organized a delegation to the White House. They informed Nixon that if he chose to go to trial he would almost certainly be convicted and removed from office.

Resignation

On August 8, 1974, Nixon appeared on national television from the Oval Office for the last time. "I have never been a quitter," Nixon said. "To leave office before

Richard Nixon says good-bye to the White House staff on August 9, 1974, after his resignation as president. Behind him are his wife Pat, daughter Tricia, and son-in-law Ed Cox.

my term is completed is abhorrent to every instinct in my body. But as president, I must put the interest of America first. Therefore I shall resign the presidency effective at noon tomorrow."

Nixon explained he was resigning because he didn't want the country and Congress to become embroiled for months in impeachment proceedings, unable to move forward in other matters vital to the nation. He admitted he had made mistakes in judgment, but that "they were made in what I believed at the time to be the best interest of the nation." What he did not say was that if he refused to resign, he would be removed by impeachment and might be tried for criminal offenses.

The next morning, Nixon woke at six o'clock. After breakfast, he gave an emotional farewell address to the White House staff. The staff applauded him warmly, and some were weeping. Throughout his speech, Nixon wiped sweat from his face, at times pausing to fight back tears. When he was finished, he and his family headed toward the waiting helicopter.

As Richard Nixon left the White House, he surely must have been cringing at this legacy, to be the first United States president ever to resign his office. But perhaps he was also thinking ahead to how to redeem himself. Although there would be no more political offices, there could still be another comeback. As he said in his farewell speech, "We think that when we suffer a defeat that all is ended. . . . Not true. It is just a beginning, always."

Chapter 6

Pardon

When the Nixons arrived at El Toro Marine Base in California, a crowd of some 5,000 supporters began to sing "God Bless America." The crowd waved and sang and cried. One voice called out, "Whittier's still for you, Dick."

Moved by the support, Nixon gave an impromptu speech. "I am going to continue to work for peace [throughout] all the world," he said. "I intend to continue to work for opportunity and understanding among the people in America." Indeed, Nixon would spend much of the rest of his life doing just those things, but he had his work cut out for him. Outside of his small band of supporters, the country was hostile toward Nixon. He and Pat spent most of their first 18 months in self-imposed exile at La Casa Pacifica, their estate in San Clemente.

A month after Nixon resigned, President Ford addressed the nation. He announced he was giving Nixon a "full, free, and absolute

President Gerald Ford announces his decision to give Richard Nixon a full and unconditional pardon during a televised appearance on September 8, 1974.

pardon" for any offenses he might have committed in office. This meant Nixon could no longer be prosecuted on criminal charges. Ford said he was granting the pardon in order to save the country from being further torn apart by the Watergate scandal. Ford also knew that Nixon himself was depressed and ill and may have believed that Nixon had suffered enough.

Many Americans were shocked and angered by Ford's pardon of Nixon. Some suggested that Nixon had struck a deal before leaving Washington: He would

What Happened to the Tapes?

From the moment Richard Nixon resigned, he was embroiled in a legal battle for the rights to his presidential papers and tapes. Every other president had taken his papers with him when he left the White House, and Nixon wanted the same right. Congress had other ideas. In December 1974, it passed the Presidential Recordings and Materials Preservation Act, and President Ford signed it into law. The act granted the government "complete possession and control" of Nixon's presidential materials. Nixon challenged the bill in court, saying that the act singled him out and treated him differently from other presidents. The case went to the Supreme Court, which upheld the act.

Nixon's presidential materials remain in the possession of the National Archives near Washington, D.C. Over the years, it has released batches of tapes to the public, who still clamor to listen to the private conversations of Richard Nixon.

☆★☆

agree to resign in exchange for a pardon. There is no evidence that such a bargain was struck. It is clear, however, that Ford's popularity suffered a serious decline. The pardon may have cost him election to a full term as president in 1976.

Rehabilitation

After a serious bout with phlebitis (inflammation of the blood vessels in his legs), Nixon underwent surgery in October 1974. He returned home two weeks later, tired and drained. Gradually, as his health improved and the nation's anger cooled, he returned to his busy schedule.

For many years, he continued to travel overseas as an unofficial ambassador, visiting with foreign leaders and receiving honor and respect. Many outside the United States saw him as a brilliant statesman and believed that his misdeeds in the Watergate scandal were small compared to his achievements. In 1978, a French reporter said, "It's too bad he can't run for president of France. He would win hands down." Among Republican leaders at home, Nixon became an *elder statesman*, unofficially advising a succession of Republican presidents, including Gerald Ford, Ronald Reagan, and the first George Bush.

Nixon also spent much of his time writing. Beginning with his hefty memoirs, published in 1978, he wrote ten books about peace and foreign policy.

They received wide attention, and several became best sellers. In addition, he contributed articles to magazines.

Endings

Richard and Pat Nixon moved to an elegant apartment in New York City in 1980 to be closer to their children. Later they moved to a handsome home in a nearby New Jersey suburb. They continued to visit California, however.

On June 19, 1990, they attended the dedication of the Richard Nixon Library and Birthplace in Yorba Linda. President George H. W. Bush was there to celebrate Nixon's legacy, along with former presidents Ford and Reagan and thousands of supporters and well-wishers. At the end of his remarks, President Bush addressed Nixon directly, saying, "History will say of you, 'Here was a true architect of peace.'"

In 1993, one day after their 53rd wedding anniversary, Pat Nixon died of lung cancer. Less than a year later, Nixon suffered a stroke. He slipped into a coma and never regained consciousness. He died in New York City on April 22, 1994.

Nearly 50,000 people came to pay their respects to the former president. They waited in lines for up to 18 hours to pass his coffin. Leaders from around the world attended the funeral, as did every living U.S. president. Richard Nixon was

In 1990, nearly 16 years after leaving the White House, Richard Nixon speaks at the dedication of his presidential library in Yorba Linda, California. Behind him are three Republican presidents who served after he left office: Ronald Reagan, George Bush, and Gerald Ford (with back to camera).

buried next to Pat at the Nixon Library and Birthplace, near the small white house in Yorba Linda where he was born.

An Unsettled Legacy ———————————————

Richard Nixon left office as one of the most unpopular presidents in history. His conduct in the Watergate affair made it easy to portray him as a deceiver, and his conversations in the Watergate tapes made him seem mean-spirited and vengeful, especially in dealing with his political "enemies."

Yet as the shock of Watergate recedes into the past, historians have begun to recall his many achievements as president. A brilliant politician and statesman, Nixon succeeded in ending U.S. involvement in the Vietnam conflict, opened relations with China, signed the first treaty limiting production of nuclear arms with the Soviet Union, and paved the way for peace between Egypt and Israel. At home he had a hand in establishing greater concern for the environment and for worker safety. His unrealized plans included reorganization of the government to make it more efficient and less expensive.

Nixon was a complicated man who, like all humans, had bad traits interlaced with good. As president, he succeeded brilliantly at many things, but never quite controlled his dark, suspicious side. As political journalist Daniel Schorr put it, "He'll be remembered as one who could have been—*could* have been—one of our great presidents. Except he did himself in."

It is still too soon to know how history will finally judge Richard Nixon. He will never lose the mark of Watergate, but it may not permanently overshadow his accomplishments. Evaluating his presidency will always involve finding a balance between his great gifts and his great weaknesses.

Fast Facts Richard Milhous Nixon

Birth:	January 9, 1913
Birthplace:	Yorba Linda, California
Parents:	Francis Anthony Nixon (known as Frank) and Hannah Milhous Nixon
Brothers:	Harold Samuel (1909–1933) Arthur Burdg (1918–1925) Francis Donald (1914–1987) Edward Calvert (1930–)
Education:	Whittier College, graduated 1934 Duke University Law School, graduated 1937
Occupation:	Lawyer
Marriage:	To Thelma "Pat" Ryan, June 21, 1940
Children:	(*see* First Lady Fast Facts at right)
Political Party:	Republican
Public Offices:	1947–1951 U.S. House of Representatives 1951–1953 U.S. Senate 1953–1961 Vice President of the United States 1969–1974 Thirty-seventh President of the United States
His Vice Presidents:	Spiro Agnew (resigned October 1973) Gerald Ford (December 1973–January 1977)
Major Actions as President:	1970 Established the Environmental Protection Agency 1970 Established the Occupational Safety and Health Administration 1972 Visited Communist China, began to regularize U.S. relations 1972 Signed SALT agreement with Soviet Union 1973 Announced the cease-fire in Vietnam 1973 Ended the military draft 1973 Signed the Endangered Species Act 1973 Signed the Prevention of Nuclear War Treaty 1974 Resigned as president
Firsts:	First (and only) person to be elected twice as vice president and twice as president First (and only) person to be nominated five times to a national ticket (twice as vice president; three times as president) First U.S. president to visit China First U.S. president to enter the Kremlin in Moscow First (and only) U.S. president to resign from office
Death:	April 22, 1994
Age at Death:	81 years
Burial Place:	The Richard Nixon Library & Birthplace, Yorba Linda, California

Fast Facts

Thelma Catherine "Pat" Ryan

Birth:	March 16, 1912
Birthplace:	Ely, Nevada
Parents:	William Ryan Sr. and Kate Halberstadt Ryan
Sisters & Brothers:	Mathew Bender, half-brother (1907–?)
	Neva Bender, half-sister (1909–?)
	William Jr. (1910–1997)
	Thomas (1911–1992)
Education:	University of Southern California, graduated 1937
Marriage:	To Richard M. Nixon, June 21, 1940
Children:	Tricia (1946–)
	Julie (1948–)
Firsts:	First to have a child married in the Rose Garden
Death:	June 22, 1993
Age at Death:	81 years
Burial Place:	The Richard Nixon Library & Birthplace, Yorba Linda, California

Timeline

1913
Richard Milhous Nixon born in Yorba Linda, California, January 9.

1922
Nixon family moves to Whittier, California.

1930
Nixon graduates from Whittier High School.

1934
Graduates form Whittier College.

1937
Graduates from Duke University Law School.

1948
As a leader of the House Un-American Activities Committee, exposes Alger Hiss.

1950
Elected to the U.S. Senate from California.

1952
Elected vice president, with President Dwight D. Eisenhower.

1956
Re-elected vice president with President Eisenhower.

1959
Represents the United States in Moscow, engages Soviet premier Khrushchev in the "kitchen debate."

1972
Visits China and "opens" it to U.S. diplomatic and economic relations.

1972
Signs the SALT agreement with the Soviet Union, limiting strategic weapons for the first time.

1972
Five burglars arrested in the Democratic National Committee office at the Watergate complex.

1972
Nixon re-elected president of the United States.

1973
Announces the Paris Peace Accords, ending direct U.S. military involvement in the Vietnam War.

1937	1940	1942	1945	1946
Admitted to California state bar; begins law practice in Whittier.	Marries Thelma "Pat" Ryan, June 21.	Joins U.S. Navy.	Discharged from U.S. Navy as a lieutenant commander.	Elected to the U.S. House of Representatives from California.

1960	1962	1963	1968	1971
Defeated in presidential election by John F. Kennedy.	Defeated in election for California governorship by Edmund G. Brown.	Enters private law practice in New York City.	Elected the 37th president of the United States.	Twenty-sixth Amendment changes voting age to 18.

1973	1974	1993	1994
Vice president Spiro Agnew resigns; Nixon nominates Gerald Ford to succeed him.	Nixon resigns to avoid impeachment proceedings in the Watergate affair, August 9.	Pat Nixon dies in Park Ridge, New Jersey, June 22.	Nixon dies in New York City, April 22.

Glossary

Communism: a political system in which the government controls all property, industries, and businesses in the name of the people

counsel: a lawyer who provides advice or represents a client in legal proceedings

détente: an easing of tensions or strain, especially between countries

elder statesman: a retired politician or government official who serves as an unofficial adviser to current leaders

executive privilege: a president's claim of the right to keep discussions with advisers confidential

impeachment: in U.S. government, a procedure in which a high official can be charged with serious wrongdoing, tried, and if found guilty, removed from office

internationalist: a person who believes that his or her country should be closely involved with other nations

neutral: not aligned with either side in a war or dispute

pacifist: a person who opposes fighting in or supporting any war

perjury: the crime of lying in official testimony after swearing to tell the truth

segregation: the separation of a group of people from other groups by law; in the southern United States, African Americans were long segregated from white citizens

subpoena: an official demand from a court of law for documents or testimony from a person or organization

subversive: a person who holds antigovernment views and may seek to undermine the government's activities

Further Reading

★ ★ ★ ★ ★

Barr, Roger. *Richard Nixon*. San Diego, CA: Lucent Books, 1992.

Barron, Rachel. *Richard Nixon: American Politician*. Greensboro, NC: Morgan Reynolds, 2004.

Feinberg, Barbara S. *Patricia Ryan Nixon, 1912–1993*. New York: Children's Press, 1998.

Kilian, Pamela. *What Was Watergate?* New York: St. Martin's Press, 1990.

Schuman, Michael A. *Richard M. Nixon*. Springfield, NJ: Enslow Publishers, 1998.

MORE ADVANCED READING

Ambrose, Stephen E. *Nixon: The Education of a Politician, 1913–1962*. New York: Simon & Schuster, 1987.

———. *Nixon: The Triumph of a Politician, 1962–1972*. New York: Simon & Schuster, 1989.

———. *Nixon: Ruin and Recovery, 1973–1990*. New York: Simon & Schuster, 1991.

Greenberg, David. *Nixon's Shadow: The History of an Image*. New York: W.W. Norton, 2003.

Nixon, Richard M. *The Memoirs of Richard Nixon*. New York: Grosset & Dunlap, 1978.

Small, Melvin. *The Presidency of Richard Nixon*. Lawrence: University Press of Kansas, 1999.

Places to Visit

★ ★ ★ ★ ★

The Capitol Building
Constitution Avenue
Washington, DC 20510
(202) 225-6827 (visitor information)

Richard Nixon served here in the House
of Representatives 1947–1951 and in the
Senate 1951–1953.

The Richard Nixon Library and Birthplace
18001 Yorba Linda Boulevard
Yorba Linda, CA 92886
(714) 993-5075
http://www.nixonfoundation.org/

Visit the house in which Richard Nixon was
born, the grave sites of Richard and Pat
Nixon, and a museum dedicated to his life
and achievements. The Nixon Library and
Birthplace is privately run and not affiliated
with the government.

Vietnam Veterans Memorial
Bacon Drive and Constitution Avenue
The National Mall
Washington, DC
(202) 426-6841
http://www.nps.gov/vive/home.htm

Walk through this poignant memorial to
those killed in the Vietnam War.

The White House
1600 Pennsylvania Avenue NW
Washington, DC 20500
Visitors' Office: (202) 456-7041
http://www.whitehouse.gov
Tour the White House, Richard Nixon's
home from 1969 to 1974.

Online Sites of Interest

★ **The American Presidency**

http://ap.grolier.com

This site provides biographical information on the presidents at different reading levels, based on material in Scholastic/Grolier encyclopedias.

★ **The American President**

http://www.americanpresident.org/history

Provides valuable information on the life and times of U.S. presidents. Originally prepared from material for a public television series on the president, the site is now managed by the University of Virginia.

★ **Internet Public Library, Presidents of the United States (IPL POTUS)**

http://www.ipl.org/div/potus/rmnixon.html

Includes concise information about Nixon and his presidency, including audio and video clips.

★ **Nixon Family Home Page**

http://nixonfamily.freeservers.com/

Photographs, articles, and related links about the family of Richard and Pat Nixon.

★ **The Richard Nixon Library and Birthplace**

http://www.nixonfoundation.org/

This site provides a wealth of information, including texts of Nixon's presidential speeches and papers, a tour of the museum, current events related to the former president, and many related links.

★ **Vietnam Online**

http://www.pbs.org/wgbh/amex/vietnam/index.html

Information, statistics, and photographs about the Vietnam War. A companion to the television documentary "Vietnam: A Television History."

★ **The White House**

http://www.whitehouse.gov/history/presidents/rn37.html

Brief biographical articles on Richard and Pat Nixon, as well as on each president and first lady.

Table of Presidents

	1. George Washington	2. John Adams	3. Thomas Jefferson	4. James Madison
Took office	Apr 30 1789	Mar 4 1797	Mar 4 1801	Mar 4 1809
Left office	Mar 3 1797	Mar 3 1801	Mar 3 1809	Mar 3 1817
Birthplace	Westmoreland Co, VA	Braintree, MA	Shadwell, VA	Port Conway, VA
Birth date	Feb 22 1732	Oct 20 1735	Apr 13 1743	Mar 16 1751
Death date	Dec 14 1799	July 4 1826	July 4 1826	June 28 1836

 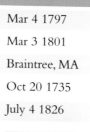 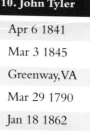 

	9. William H. Harrison	10. John Tyler	11. James K. Polk	12. Zachary Taylor
Took office	Mar 4 1841	Apr 6 1841	Mar 4 1845	Mar 5 1849
Left office	**Apr 4 1841•**	Mar 3 1845	Mar 3 1849	**July 9 1850•**
Birthplace	Berkeley, VA	Greenway, VA	Mecklenburg Co, NC	Barboursville, VA
Birth date	Feb 9 1773	Mar 29 1790	Nov 2 1795	Nov 24 1784
Death date	Apr 4 1841	Jan 18 1862	June 15 1849	July 9 1850

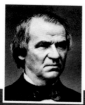 

	17. Andrew Johnson	18. Ulysses S. Grant	19. Rutherford B. Hayes	20. James A. Garfield
Took office	Apr 15 1865	Mar 4 1869	Mar 5 1877	Mar 4 1881
Left office	Mar 3 1869	Mar 3 1877	Mar 3 1881	**Sept 19 1881•**
Birthplace	Raleigh, NC	Point Pleasant, OH	Delaware, OH	Orange, OH
Birth date	Dec 29 1808	Apr 27 1822	Oct 4 1822	Nov 19 1831
Death date	July 31 1875	July 23 1885	Jan 17 1893	Sept 19 1881

5. James Monroe

Mar 4 1817

Mar 3 1825

Westmoreland Co, VA

Apr 28 1758

July 4 1831

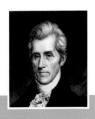

6. John Quincy Adams

Mar 4 1825

Mar 3 1829

Braintree, MA

July 11 1767

Feb 23 1848

7. Andrew Jackson

Mar 4 1829

Mar 3 1837

The Waxhaws, SC

Mar 15 1767

June 8 1845

8. Martin Van Buren

Mar 4 1837

Mar 3 1841

Kinderhook, NY

Dec 5 1782

July 24 1862

13. Millard Fillmore

July 9 1850

Mar 3 1853

Locke Township, NY

Jan 7 1800

Mar 8 1874

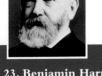

14. Franklin Pierce

Mar 4 1853

Mar 3 1857

Hillsborough, NH

Nov 23 1804

Oct 8 1869

15. James Buchanan

Mar 4 1857

Mar 3 1861

Cove Gap, PA

Apr 23 1791

June 1 1868

16. Abraham Lincoln

Mar 4 1861

Apr 15 1865•

Hardin Co, KY

Feb 12 1809

Apr 15 1865

21. Chester A. Arthur

Sept 19 1881

Mar 3 1885

Fairfield, VT

Oct 5 1829

Nov 18 1886

22. Grover Cleveland

Mar 4 1885

Mar 3 1889

Caldwell, NJ

Mar 18 1837

June 24 1908

23. Benjamin Harrison

Mar 4 1889

Mar 3 1893

North Bend, OH

Aug 20 1833

Mar 13 1901

24. Grover Cleveland

Mar 4 1893

Mar 3 1897

Caldwell, NJ

Mar 18 1837

June 24 1908

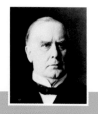

	25. William McKinley	**26. Theodore Roosevelt**	**27. William H. Taft**	**28. Woodrow Wilson**
Took office	Mar 4 1897	Sept 14 1901	Mar 4 1909	Mar 4 1913
Left office	**Sept 14 1901•**	Mar 3 1909	Mar 3 1913	Mar 3 1921
Birthplace	Niles, OH	New York, NY	Cincinnati, OH	Staunton, VA
Birth date	Jan 29 1843	Oct 27 1858	Sept 15 1857	Dec 28 1856
Death date	Sept 14 1901	Jan 6 1919	Mar 8 1930	Feb 3 1924

	33. Harry S. Truman	**34. Dwight D. Eisenhower**	**35. John F. Kennedy**	**36. Lyndon B. Johnson**
Took office	Apr 12 1945	Jan 20 1953	Jan 20 1961	Nov 22 1963
Left office	Jan 20 1953	Jan 20 1961	**Nov 22 1963•**	Jan 20 1969
Birthplace	Lamar, MO	Denison, TX	Brookline, MA	Johnson City, TX
Birth date	May 8 1884	Oct 14 1890	May 29 1917	Aug 27 1908
Death date	Dec 26 1972	Mar 28 1969	Nov 22 1963	Jan 22 1973

	41. George Bush	**42. Bill Clinton**	**43. George W. Bush**	
Took office	Jan 20 1989	Jan 20 1993	Jan 20 2001	
Left office	Jan 20 1993	Jan 20 2001	—	
Birthplace	Milton, MA	Hope, AR	New Haven, CT	
Birth date	June 12 1924	Aug 19 1946	July 6 1946	
Death date	—	—	—	

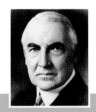
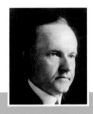

29. Warren G. Harding	30. Calvin Coolidge	31. Herbert Hoover	32. Franklin D. Roosevelt
Mar 4 1921	Aug 2 1923	Mar 4 1929	Mar 4 1933
Aug 2 1923•	Mar 3 1929	Mar 3 1933	**Apr 12 1945•**
Blooming Grove, OH	Plymouth, VT	West Branch, IA	Hyde Park, NY
Nov 21 1865	July 4 1872	Aug 10 1874	Jan 30 1882
Aug 2 1923	Jan 5 1933	Oct 20 1964	Apr 12 1945

37. Richard M. Nixon	38. Gerald R. Ford	39. Jimmy Carter	40. Ronald Reagan
Jan 20 1969	Aug 9 1974	Jan 20 1977	Jan 20 1981
Aug 9 1974★	Jan 20 1977	Jan 20 1981	Jan 20 1989
Yorba Linda, CA	Omaha, NE	Plains, GA	Tampico, IL
Jan 9 1913	July 14 1913	Oct 1 1924	Feb 11 1911
Apr 22 1994	—	—	June 5 2004

• Indicates the president died while in office.
★ Richard Nixon resigned before his term expired.

Index

Page numbers in *italics* indicate illustrations.

Agnew, Spiro, 79
American Independent Party, 56
arms control, 69

Brezhnev, Leonid, 69, *69,* 71, 76
Brown, Edmund "Pat," 48
Bush, George, 90, 91, *92*
Butterfield, Alexander, 78

Cambodia, 62, 63
Caracas, Venezuela, 42, *43*
cease-fire, 65, 75
Chambers, Whittaker, 30, *31*
Checkers speech, 37–39, *39,* 46
China, 67–69, *68,* 93
civil rights, 53
Clean Air Act, 67
Cold War, 29
Committee to Re-Elect the President, 71, 73
Communism, 26, 29, 30, 32, 42, 48, 52, 61, 75
Cox, Archibald, 78–79
Cox, Edward, 66, *84*

Dean, John, 76, *77,* 78
debate, high school, 14–15
debates, presidential, 46–48, *47,* 57
Democratic convention, *55,* 56
Democratic National Committee, 71, 73
Democratic Party, 40, 41, 75
demonstrations, political, 53, 56, 57
détente, 29, 75
Douglas, Helen Gahagan, 32, 33
draft, military, 67
Duke University, 18–19

Ehrlichman, John, *77*
Eisenhower, David, 59
Eisenhower, Dwight D., 35, *36,* 37, 38, 40-41, *41*, 48
election, 1960 presidential, 45
election, 1964 presidential, 52
election, 1968 presidential, 53
election, 1972 presidential, 64, 75
electoral college, 40, 48
Ellsberg, Daniel, 70, 71, 74
Endangered Species Act, 67
Environmental Protection Agency, 67, 93

Ford, Gerald, 7, 9, 79, 87–89, *88,* 90, 91, *92*
foreign affairs, 40, 60, 67
foreign-aid, 28

Goldwater, Barry, 51, 52
Gray, L. Patrick, *77*

Haldeman, Bob, *77*
Hiss case, 30–31, 50
House Judiciary Committee, 81, 82, 83
House of Representatives, U.S., 25–28, 32
House Un-American Activities Committee, 30
Humphrey, Hubert, 55, 56, 57
Hunt, Howard, 71, 73, 75

impeachment, 79, 82, 83, 85

Johnson, Lyndon, B., 51, 52, 53, *55*

Kennedy, John F., 45–48, *47,* 51, 52
Kent State University, 62–64, *63*
Khrushchev, Nikita, 42, 44, *44*
Kissinger, Henry, 60, *60,* 64, 70

"kitchen debate," 44
Kleindienst, Richard, *77*

Laos, 62
Liddy, G. Gordon, 71, 73, 75

Magruder, Jeb, *77*
Marshall Plan, 28
McGovern, George, 75
Middle East, 82, 93
moon landing, 65–66

New Deal, 19
New Frontier, 45–48
Nixon, Julie, 32, *49,* 59
Nixon, Pat, 25, *36,* 42, *49,* 59, *68, 84,* 91
    fast facts, 97
Nixon, Richard M., *47, 58, 92*
    campaign for governor 1962, 48
    campaign for president 1960, 45–48
    campaign for president 1968, 53, 57–59
    campaign for president 1972, 75
    Checkers speech, 37–39, *39,* 46
    debates with Kennedy, 46–48
    early life, 10–16
    education, 14–15, 16–18
    as elder statesman, 90
    family, 10, 12-14, *13,* 15–16, 17, 25, 32,
      49, 58, 59
    fast facts, 96
    and Hiss case, 30–31, 50
    and House of Representatives, U.S., 25–28,
      32
    impeachment, 79, 82, 83, 85
    inauguration, 59
    "last" press conference, 48, 50
    in law school, 18–19
    as lawyer, 23, 48, 51
    legacy, 85, 93–94

Nixon, Richard M. (cont'd.)
    marriage, 23
    in Navy, 24–25, *25*
    pardon by Ford, 87–90
    Presidential Library, *11*, 91, *92*
    and the press, 61
    resignation, 7–9, *8,* 83–85, *84*
    and Senate, 32–34
    and Soviet Union, 69
    timeline, 98–99
    as vice president, 35–44, *36*
    and Vietnam, 61–65
    visits China, 67–69
    and Watergate scandal, 73–85
    as writer, 90
Nixon, Tricia, 25, *49, 66, 84*
nuclear weapons, 69, 76, 93

Occupational Safety and Health
    Administration (OSHA), 67

pardon, 87–90, *88*
Paris Peace Accords, 65
"Pentagon Papers," 70–71
"Pink Sheets," 32
Presidential Recordings and Materials
    Preservation Act, 89
protests against U.S. in South America, 42, *43*
protests against Vietnam war, 53, *55,* 56, 57,
    59, 62, *63,* 64
"Pumpkin Papers," 30

Reagan, Ronald, 56, 90, 91, *92*
Republican National Committee, 38
Republican National Convention, 35, *36,* 56
Republican Party, 19, *25,* 26, 37, 45, 48, 51,
    53, 90
Richard Nixon Library and Birthplace, *11,*
    91, *92*

riots, 52, 53, 57
Rockefeller, Nelson, 56
Ryan, Thelma Catherine "Pat," 21–23, 97.
   See also Nixon, Pat

San Clemente, 87
Saturday Night Massacre, 79
segregation, 56
Senate, U.S., 32
Senate Watergate Committee, 78, 81
silent majority, 62
Soviet Union, 26, 29, 30, 69, 75, 93
Stevenson, Adlai, 40, 41
Strategic Arms Limitation Treaty (SALT),
   69
Supreme Court, U.S., 82

tape-recordings, 70, 74, 78, 80, *81,* 82, 89, 93
television, 38, 46-48, 83
town meetings, 57
"Tricky Dick," 32

Vietnam, 52, 53, *54,* 57, 60, 61–65, 70, 75, 93
   fast facts, 65
voting age, 67

Wallace, George, 56, 57
Watergate, 61, 71, 73–85, 89, 93
Whittier, California, 12, 15, 21, 23
Whittier College, 16–18
World War II, 24-25
   fast facts, 24
Yorba Linda, California, 10, *11,* 91, *92*

About the Author

Betsy Ochester is the author of several history books for young readers, including *John Tyler*, *Grover Cleveland*, and *George Bush* in Encyclopedia of Presidents. In addition, she has published nine titles in two Highlights for Children series, Which Way USA? and Top Secret Adventures, as well as dozens of puzzles, stories, and articles for young readers. Ms. Ochester is a graduate of Cornell University. After living in Boston, Chicago, and New York City, she now resides in Pittsburgh.